_____
Dad's Full Name

_____   _____
Date of Birth   Place of Birth

_____
Dad's Mother's Full Name

_____   _____
Date of Birth   Place of Birth

_____
Dad's Father's Full Name

_____   _____
Date of Birth   Place of Birth

MYDAD

His Stories. His Words.

WITH SPECIAL THANKS TO

Jason Aldrich, Gloria Austin, Gerry Baird, Jay Baird, Neil Beaton, Josie Bissett, Laura Boro, Chris Dalke, Jim and Alyssa Darragh & Family, Jennifer and Matt Ellison & Family, Rob Estes, Michael and Leianne Flynn & Family, Sarah Forster, Jennifer Hurwitz, Heidi Jones, Carol Anne Kennedy, June Martin, Jessica Phoenix and Tom DesLongchamp, Janet Potter & Family, Diane Roger, Christy Wires, Clarie Yam and Erik Lee, Heidi Yamada & Family, Justi and Tote Yamada & Family, Bob and Val Yamada, Kaz and Kristin Yamada & Family, Tai and Joy Yamada, Anne Zadra, August and Arline Zadra, and Gus and Rosie Zadra.

CREDITS

Compiled by Dan Zadra & Kristel Wills
Designed by Steve Potter
Created by Kobi Yamada

ISBN: 978-1-932319-64-4
©2008 by Compendium, Incorporated. All rights reserved. No part of this publication may be reproduced or transmitted in any form or by any means, electronic or mechanical, including photocopy, recording, or any storage and retrieval system now known or to be invented without written permission from the publisher. Contact: Compendium, Inc., 600 North 36th Street, Suite 400, Seattle, WA 98103. My Dad, His Stories. His Words., Compendium, live inspired and the format, design, layout and coloring used in this book are trademarks and/or trade dress of Compendium, Incorporated. This book may be ordered directly from the publisher, but please try your local bookstore first. Call us at 800-91-IDEAS or come see our full line of inspiring products at www.live-inspired.com.

1st Printing. 7500 01 08   Printed in China

DEAR**DAD**...

In your hands you hold one of the most thoughtful gifts you could ever give your family. It won't take long for you to respond to the questions in this little book, but future generations will treasure your answers forever.

Imagine if your grandfather had been able to tuck away a similar book for you. What a joy to discover a few of his favorite memories of the old days, in his own handwriting. Well, now is your chance to pick up a pen and create a wonderful family heirloom of your own.

Like a trip down memory lane, the following pages will whisk you back to another time and place. The questions are simple and straightforward, but only you can provide the answers—and that's what makes this book so special.

When you were a child, what did you want to be when you grew up? What was your old neighborhood like? Who were your best friends? Have fun with your answers— they don't need to be formal or complicated. Just answer straight from the heart, and the result is sure to be magical to those who love you.

DAD, what kind of house did you grow up in, and what was the old neighborhood like?

_____

_____

_____

_____

_____

_____

_____

_____

_____

DAD, when you were a kid, what was your favorite holiday, and how did your family celebrate it?

_____

_____

_____

_____

_____

_____

_____

_____

_____

DAD, which were your favorite pets, and what made them special?

_____

_____

_____

_____

_____

_____

_____

_____

_____

_____

DAD, what's your favorite memory of your dad? Your mom?

_____

_____

_____

_____

_____

_____

_____

_____

_____

DAD, what's the best thing your dad and/or mom taught you?

_____

_____

_____

_____

_____

_____

_____

_____

_____

DAD, what rules did your parents have, and which ones drove you crazy?

_____

_____

_____

_____

_____

_____

_____

_____

_____

_____

DAD, what are one or two things you did that you didn't tell your parents about?

_____

_____

_____

_____

_____

_____

_____

_____

_____

_____

DAD, what was your relationship like with your family when you were growing up?

_____

_____

_____

_____

_____

_____

_____

_____

_____

DAD, what traits do you have that your parents also had? And which side of your family do you most resemble?

_____

_____

_____

_____

_____

_____

_____

_____

_____

DAD, when you were a child, what did you want to be when you grew up? When you were a teenager? When you were a young adult?

_____

_____

_____

_____

_____

_____

_____

_____

_____

DAD, who were your best friends from childhood, and what were they like?

_____

_____

_____

_____

_____

_____

_____

_____

_____

_____

DAD, what music did you grow up listening to?

_____

_____

_____

_____

_____

_____

_____

_____

_____

_____

DAD, what were your favorite subjects in school, and why?

_____

_____

_____

_____

_____

_____

_____

_____

_____

DAD, who was your favorite teacher, and why?

_____

_____

_____

_____

_____

_____

_____

_____

_____

_____

DAD, did you play a sport, and what did you like best about it?

_____

_____

_____

_____

_____

_____

_____

_____

_____

DAD, who taught you to drive, and what was your first car?

_____

_____

_____

_____

_____

_____

_____

_____

_____

DAD, did you ever win an award you were proud of, and what was it in honor of?

_____

_____

_____

_____

_____

_____

_____

_____

_____

DAD, what was the worst trouble you got into when you were younger?

_____

_____

_____

_____

_____

_____

_____

_____

_____

DAD, what were your first few jobs? What did you do, and do you remember how much you earned?

_____

_____

_____

_____

_____

_____

_____

_____

_____

DAD, what was your toughest lesson in life?

_____

_____

_____

_____

_____

_____

_____

_____

_____

DAD, what is the best advice you ever received, and from whom?

_____

_____

_____

_____

_____

_____

_____

_____

_____

DAD, how did you meet Mom?

_____

_____

_____

_____

_____

_____

_____

_____

_____

DAD, how did you spend your free time before you had kids?

_____

_____

_____

_____

_____

_____

_____

_____

_____

DAD, what do you remember about the birth of your children?

_____

_____

_____

_____

_____

_____

_____

_____

_____

DAD, what was it like to become a father?

_____

_____

_____

_____

_____

_____

_____

_____

_____

DAD, what is one of your favorite memories of being a dad?

_____

_____

_____

_____

_____

_____

_____

_____

_____

DAD, what are some of your favorite things you've done with your children?

_____

_____

_____

_____

_____

_____

_____

_____

_____

DAD, what's the best thing about being a father?
What's the hardest thing?

_____

_____

_____

_____

_____

_____

_____

_____

_____

_____

DAD, what advice would you pass along about being a dad?

_____

_____

_____

_____

_____

_____

_____

_____

_____

DAD, looking back, what are some of your proudest
moments in life?

_____

_____

_____

_____

_____

_____

_____

_____

_____

_____

DAD, who are the people that you most admire, and why?

_____

_____

_____

_____

_____

_____

_____

_____

_____

_____

DAD, what's your favorite motto, quotation or saying? Where did you hear it?

_____

_____

_____

_____

_____

_____

_____

_____

_____

_____

DAD, where is the most interesting place you've ever visited, and why?

_____

_____

_____

_____

_____

_____

_____

_____

_____

DAD, what are some ways—good and bad—the world has changed since you were a kid?

_____

_____

_____

_____

_____

_____

_____

_____

_____

DAD, what's the craziest or most impulsive thing you've ever done?

_____

_____

_____

_____

_____

_____

_____

_____

_____

_____

DAD, what is your perfect day?

_____

_____

_____

_____

_____

_____

_____

_____

_____

DAD, what are some things that you still want to do
in your lifetime?

_____

_____

_____

_____

_____

_____

_____

_____

_____

_____

DAD, how do you want future generations of your family to remember you?

_____

_____

_____

_____

_____

_____

_____

_____

_____

MEMORIES ARE OUR GREATEST INHERITANCE.

—Peter Hamill